A Child's First Library of Learning

Animals in Action

TIME LIFE ASIA

Contents

❓ Do Moths and Butterflies Have Eyes on Their Wings?

ANSWER ◆ Some moths have markings on their rear wings that look like large eyes. Usually the moth hides them, but when it is attacked the moth shows them to frighten the attacker.

Here it is.

The bird was going to eat the moth until it saw the markings shaped like large eyes. When those suddenly appeared, the bird was frightened and flew away.

■ The hawk moth

The eye-shaped markings of the hawk moth usually cannot be seen because they are hidden by the moth's front wings. And since the front wings are the same colour as the leaves of a tree, the moth can blend in with its surroundings. But when the moth moves its front wings the eye-shaped markings appear suddenly, and this frightens away an attacker.

▲ **With front wings closed**   ▲ **With front wings spread apart**

Aha! Food!

This bird has spotted a butterfly.

ANSWER 2 Some butterflies have small eye-shaped markings on their wings. An attacker will think the markings are the butterfly's head and will peck at them. But since it hasn't really been pecked in the head, the butterfly can escape.

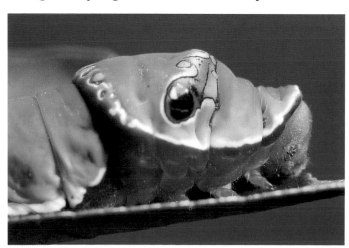

The bird pecks at the eye shaped markings instead of the real eyes.

Even though its wing is torn the butterfly escapes by flying away.

Caterpillars with Eye-shaped Markings

Markings that look like eyes are found not only on butterflies and moths. Some caterpillars have them too. When an attacker appears the caterpillar curls up so that the large, eye-like markings appear. That generally frightens the attacker away.

This upside-down one seems to have two eyes.

This hawk moth caterpillar looks like a snake.

Black swallowtail caterpillar. It has eye-like markings on the part of its body called the thorax.

● **To the Parent**

The eye-like markings on some butterflies and moths serve different purposes according to their size. Large eye-like markings frighten away attackers. Small eye-like markings present false eyes to an enemy to lure it away from the true eyes. Birds are scared off by the large eye-shaped markings but they will aim their attacks at the smaller markings. Some caterpillars also have large eye-like markings to frighten off attackers. Explain to your child that caterpillars turn into butterflies and moths.

Why Does This Caterpillar Have Horns?

ANSWER This is a swallowtail caterpillar. If something touches it or shakes the branch that it is on, the caterpillar puts out yellow horns that give off a bad smell. That is the way it protects itself from enemies. Whatever is attacking the caterpillar is driven away by the awful-smelling horns.

▲ The swallowtail caterpillar has horns that give off a bad smell.

The Secrets of the Swallowtail Caterpillar's Body

The caterpillar is very different from the butterfly it will turn into. Let's take a close look to see just how it is different.

The real eyes are very small, and there are six of them on either side of the head.

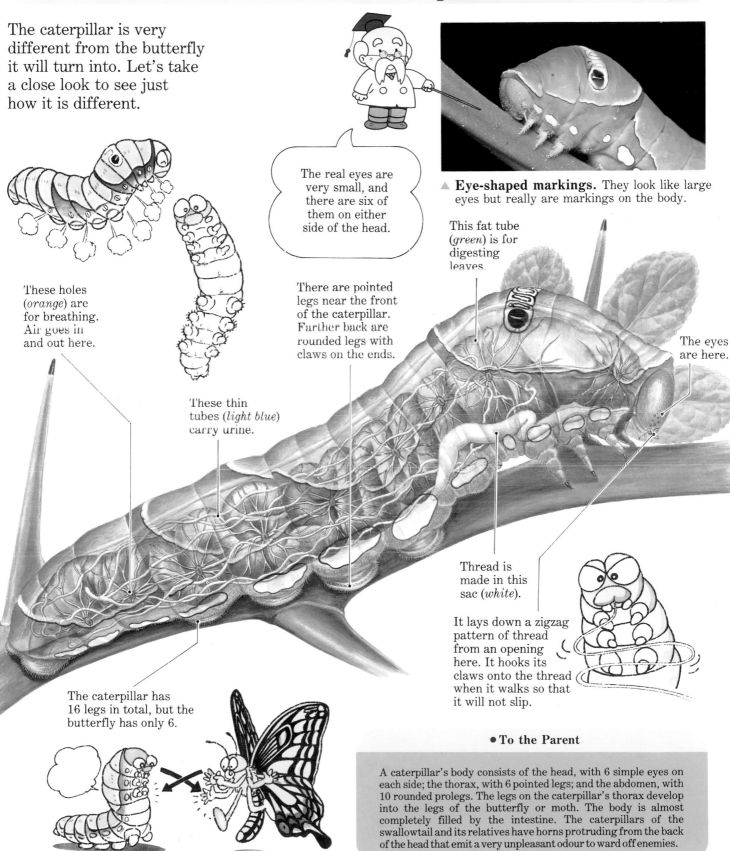

▲ **Eye-shaped markings.** They look like large eyes but really are markings on the body.

This fat tube (*green*) is for digesting leaves.

These holes (*orange*) are for breathing. Air goes in and out here.

There are pointed legs near the front of the caterpillar. Farther back are rounded legs with claws on the ends.

The eyes are here.

These thin tubes (*light blue*) carry urine.

Thread is made in this sac (*white*).

It lays down a zigzag pattern of thread from an opening here. It hooks its claws onto the thread when it walks so that it will not slip.

The caterpillar has 16 legs in total, but the butterfly has only 6.

● **To the Parent**

A caterpillar's body consists of the head, with 6 simple eyes on each side; the thorax, with 6 pointed legs; and the abdomen, with 10 rounded prolegs. The legs on the caterpillar's thorax develop into the legs of the butterfly or moth. The body is almost completely filled by the intestine. The caterpillars of the swallowtail and its relatives have horns protruding from the back of the head that emit a very unpleasant odour to ward off enemies.

Why Do Dragonflies Fly Around in the Same Place?

(ANSWER) They are protecting their territory. The male silver dragonfly claims an area where the female can lay her eggs. Then he patrols that territory, and if any other males come into it he chases them away.

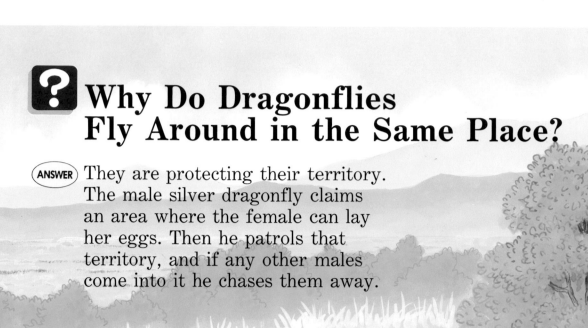

Female silver dragonfly

Male silver dragonfly

I'm with her!

I'll rest.

▲ **Male silver dragonfly.** He flies with his legs tucked in. The male's body is green and blue. The female's body is just green.

Let's get together.

Hey! A rival moving in!

Get out of here! This is my territory.

I'm going.

Whew!

● **To the Parent**

The males of some dragonfly species stake out territory and protect it. The silver dragonfly is one such species. It is often seen near water. The male will attack other males to keep them away from his territory, but if a female approaches he mates with her and she lays her eggs in the water while they are still joined together. A male silver dragonfly defends territory that usually is about 65 to 100 feet (20 to 30 m) in diameter.

? Why Do Some Bugs Stink?

ANSWER ▶ That awful smell protects them from their enemies. When a stink bug is attacked it sprays liquid from holes in its body. The liquid turns into a mist that smells terrible. When other insects breathe in the mist their bodies begin to shiver and shake.

Spray holes

Liquid comes out of holes near the middle legs.

▲ **Protecting its eggs.** When a spider comes near, the stink bug sprays out a smelly mist.

ANSWER 2 The smell also lets other stink bugs know that danger is near. If one of the bugs is attacked by an enemy, it sprays its smelly liquid. The others will run away as fast as they can after they have smelt the warning spray.

Stink bugs and skunks use an unpleasant smell for protection.

•To the Parent

Stink bugs produce an odour so revolting it is hard to describe. The awful smell comes from odour glands that secrete a liquid. It can make leaves or fruit that stink bugs have rested on taste bad. Sprayed out through holes located where the middle legs join the body, the liquid becomes a mist with a foul smell that drives away enemies. The smell has no effect, however, on some attackers such as praying mantises, chickens and frogs. Some kinds of stink bugs use the spray to protect their eggs and larvae. And some kinds of stink bugs found living in colonies use their smelly spray to warn other members of the colony of an attack. There are over 5,000 different species of stink bugs found around the world.

? Why Do Cicadas Sing?

(ANSWER) The male cicadas are the ones that sing. They do it to attract mates. When a male is singing, not only females but other males gather around. Once the males and females have gathered, they find partners that suit them, then they mate.

Brown cicada

? How Do Cicadas Make Sounds?

They use a special sound-making organ that is inside their stomach. The sounds are made by muscles and a membrane on the bottom of the male cicada's stomach. When the muscles vibrate the membrane it makes a small sound, which becomes much louder after it echoes inside a space in the cicada's stomach.

Inside the cicada's stomach

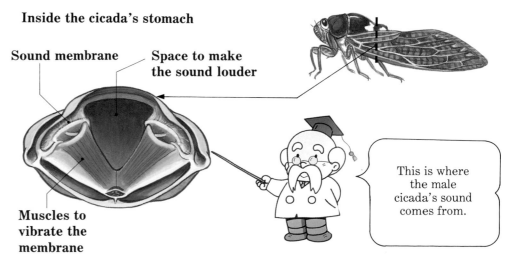

Sound membrane

Space to make the sound louder

Muscles to vibrate the membrane

This is where the male cicada's sound comes from.

12

Kaempfer cicada

Which way?

▲ **Kaempfer cicada.** The male sings as the female above starts to pay attention to him.

Making a Toy Cicada Out of Bamboo

You can make toy cicadas out of bamboo. First, make a tiny drum from bamboo and paper. Then put pine resin on a stick and attach the drum to it with string. When you twirl the toy the string rubs against the resin and makes a small sound. The string carries the sound to the drum, which makes it louder.

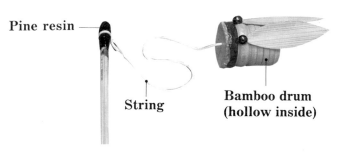

Pine resin

String

Bamboo drum (hollow inside)

● **To the Parent**

Male cicadas produce different kinds of sounds. One sound is a congregational call that attracts both females and other males. Another sound is produced when the male cicada approaches, or courts, a female. And yet another sound is heard when the male cicada is in distress, as when he has been captured by people.

13

Why Do Crickets Chirp?

ANSWER 1 Only the male crickets make sounds. In that way they are like cicadas. The cricket you see here makes three different kinds of chirping sounds. He uses one of those to keep other males out of his territory.

ANSWER 2 When the male cricket is trying to attract a female, he uses another kind of sound. The male tries to make the female take a liking to him with his special chirping song.

These male crickets make yet another kind of chirping sound when they are fighting each other. As they chirp they butt their heads together. When one gives up and runs away, the noise stops.

● **To the Parent**

Crickets, katydids and long-horned grasshoppers make their chirping sounds by rubbing their front wings together. Short-horned grasshoppers, which include locusts, make their chirping sounds by rubbing their back legs and their wings together. Typically, only the male of the species chirps. There are a few species, though, in which the female can make a faint chirp.

How Insects Make Their Chirping Sounds

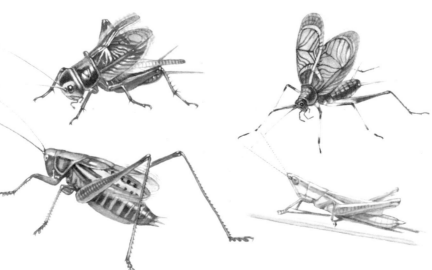

Cricket
He raises his two front wings slightly and rubs them together.

Japanese katydid
He raises his two front wings up high and rubs them together.

Katydid
He raises his two front wings only a very little and rubs them together.

Locust
He rubs his back legs and wings together.

❓ Did You Know That Some Ants Steal Young Ants from Other Nests?

ANSWER Slave-making ants keep black ants as slaves. The slave-making ants raid black ants' nests and steal the unborn ants, which are called pupae. They take these back to their own nest, where the pupae become adult ants and spend their lives serving their captors.

Inside a Slave-making Ant Nest

The black ants do all the work because they think it is really their own nest.

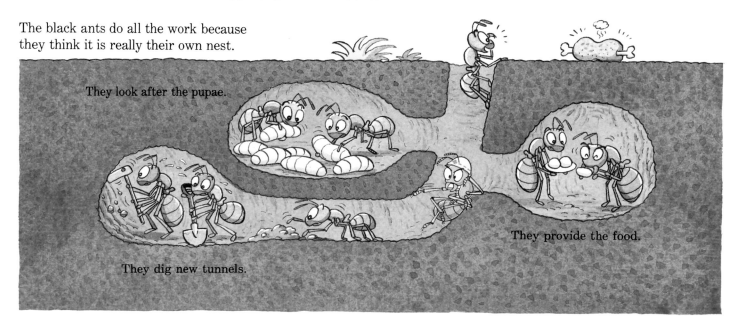

They look after the pupae.

They dig new tunnels.

They provide the food.

■ The body of a slave-making ant

▲ **Face of a slave-making ant**

Because their jaws are so large, they cannot eat without help. So they get black ants to feed them.

They use their strong jaws to hold and carry away the pupae when they raid a nest of black ants.

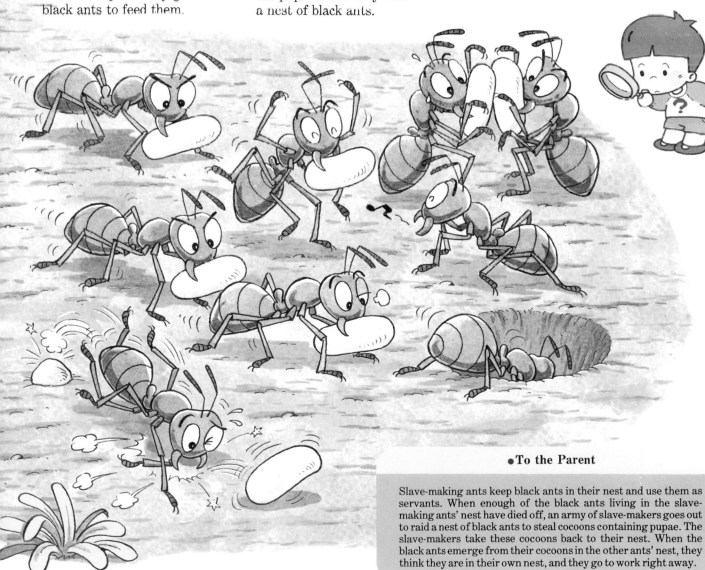

● **To the Parent**

Slave-making ants keep black ants in their nest and use them as servants. When enough of the black ants living in the slave-making ants' nest have died off, an army of slave-makers goes out to raid a nest of black ants to steal cocoons containing pupae. The slave-makers take these cocoons back to their nest. When the black ants emerge from their cocoons in the other ants' nest, they think they are in their own nest, and they go to work right away.

❓ What Does a Tumblebug Eat?

ANSWER The tumblebug eats dung. This is the waste left by larger animals. It makes round balls of dung so that it can roll them to a place where it is safe to eat them.

Whenever they pick up the smell of dung, large numbers of tumblebugs come from all around.

They take small pieces from a lump of dung until they have formed a round ball.

▲ **Tumblebug rolling a ball of dung.** It uses its front legs to support its body and move along while it rolls the ball with its middle and back legs.

■ A tumblebug having a meal

The tumblebug has to watch out for enemies and competitors in places where dung is found.

They dig holes in the earth and eat their food underground.

▲ A yellow baboon is one of the tumblebug's enemies. The baboon breaks up pieces of dung and eats insects it finds.

■ Providing food for their young

The tumblebug buries a pear-shaped lump of dung in the ground and lays an egg inside it. When the larva hatches it will eat the dung.

▲ Eggs are laid in pear-shaped balls of dung. Here the surface has been scraped away to show the egg inside.

A chamber is dug 16 to 20 inches (40 to 50 cm) below ground, and balls of dung are laid on their side in the nest.

● To the Parent

Insects that live on the manure of animals are called dung beetles. One of these is the tumblebug, a dung beetle that feeds on the dung of herbivorous animals. The tumblebug rolls the dung into balls that can be as large as apples. The tumblebug feeds on these balls and lays its eggs in them. When a larva hatches, it stays inside the ball and feeds on the dung while it matures. Dung beetles can eat more than their own weight in 24 hours.

? How Do Spiders Spin Webs?

ANSWER In a spider's web some of the threads are sticky and some are not. The spider first spins the framework of the web with threads that are not sticky and uses those as a foothold. Then it spins the rest of the web with threads that are extremely sticky.

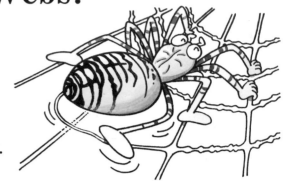

It spins sticky spiral threads.

■ Spinning a web

—— **Nonsticky thread**   —— **Foothold thread**   —— **Sticky thread**

① First the spider spins the topmost thread of the web.

② Hanging by a thread, it spins three threads like spokes.

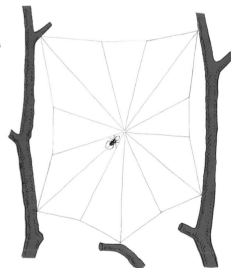

③ Then it adds the outer frame and more threads as spokes.

④ It adds foothold threads to use while spinning spiral threads.

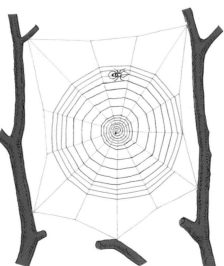

⑤ As it adds the sticky spirals it cuts the foothold threads away.

⑥ When the sticky spirals go almost to the centre, the web is finished.

The centre does not catch anything.

▲ **Web of a golden spider.** The spider waits in the centre of the web, where the threads are not sticky.

Some of the Webs That Spiders Spin

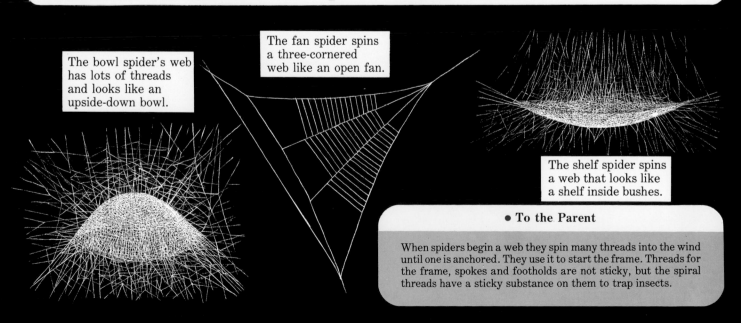

The bowl spider's web has lots of threads and looks like an upside-down bowl.

The fan spider spins a three-cornered web like an open fan.

The shelf spider spins a web that looks like a shelf inside bushes.

● **To the Parent**

When spiders begin a web they spin many threads into the wind until one is anchored. They use it to start the frame. Threads for the frame, spokes and footholds are not sticky, but the spiral threads have a sticky substance on them to trap insects.

Where Is the Mouth of a Starfish?

ANSWER A starfish's mouth is on the underside of its body. The mouth is the opening in the centre where the five arms meet. When a starfish wants to eat, its stomach comes out through the mouth, closes over the prey and digests it.

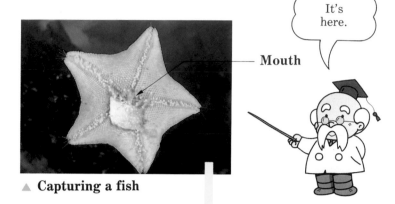

▲ Capturing a fish

Mouth

It's here.

▲ **A starfish digesting a fish.** The light-coloured stomach emerges from the mouth to digest the food.

22

And What Do Starfish Eat?

▲ A starfish eating a clam

Starfish eat fish, clams and other shellfish.

▲ Spider starfish eating tiny sea animals

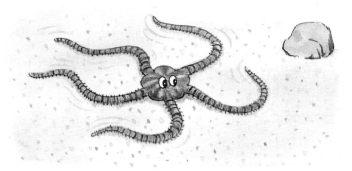

The spider starfish eats very small creatures that it finds on the sand or on rocks.

▲ Crown-of-thorns starfish eating coral

This one eats the small animals that form coral.

The crown-of-thorns starfish has poisonous spikes.

● To the Parent

A starfish has tubular feet with suction pads on the ends for attaching the feet to objects. To eat a bivalve shellfish, such as a clam, the starfish uses its suction feet to pull at the shell until it opens. The mouth of the starfish is located in the centre of its underside. There are no teeth or tentacles in the mouth. Instead the starfish uses an unusual method of digestion in which it turns its stomach inside out, envelops the prey and then digests the prey outside its body. When the starfish is done, it retracts its stomach.

How Do Sea Anemones Catch Fish?

ANSWER The tentacles of a sea anemone have poisonous spines in them. When a fish touches one of the tentacles it gets stabbed by many poisonous spines and cannot move. Then the anemone uses its tentacles to pull the fish in.

▲ A sea anemone catches a small fish.

The sea anemone spreads out its tentacles and waits for a fish to come along.

When a fish touches the tentacles, poisonous spines come out and touch the fish. The poison makes the fish unable to move.

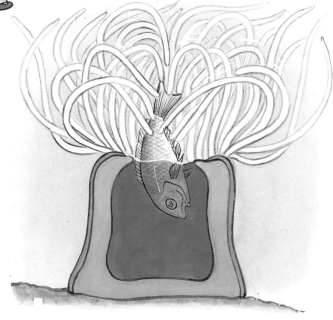

When the fish stops moving, the anemone pulls it inside its body and digests it.

The secret of the poisonous spines

The poisonous spines are located in small sacs in the tentacles. When something disturbs a sac, the spine pops out suddenly.

Like a blowpipe!

When it cannot eat any more, it pushes the leftovers outside.

24

Then Why Doesn't the Anemone Fish Get Hurt?

The anemone fish lives all its life very near the sea anemone. But the fish is perfectly all right even when it bumps against the tentacles. The fish's body is covered with a film that protects it against the sea anemone's poisonous spines.

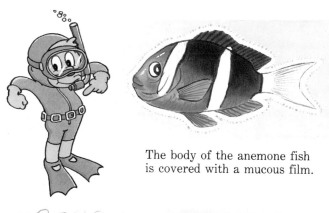

The body of the anemone fish is covered with a mucous film.

▲ The anemone fish lives around the sea anemone.

The poisonous spines of the sea anemone cannot pass through this mucous film, so the anemone fish is safe.

 MINI-DATA

What would happen if the film of mucus were wiped off the anemone fish's body? If that happened it would lose its protection and be just like other fish. The poisonous spines would sting it and the sea anemone would eat it.

The anemone fish gets away from its attackers by hiding in the safety of the sea anemone's tentacles.

●To the Parent

The sea anemone and the jellyfish belong to the phylum Cnidaria, whose members are characterized by stinging cells called nematocysts. When the nematocysts are stimulated, for example by a fish brushing against them, the stinging nettle coiled inside each nematocyst pops out, pierces the offender's skin and injects a poison that is paralysing. The immobilized fish is then ingested.

How Do Salmon Return to Where They Were Born?

ANSWER Salmon spend most of their life in the ocean, but they return to the river where they were born when it is time to lay eggs. Salmon can remember the smell of the river they originally came from. Once they find it, they swim up it and spawn.

Here's mine.

Which one is mine?

A salmon jumps in the mouth of a river. Once their bodies are used to the fresh water they start upstream.

How Can They Find Their Way in the Ocean?

Once a salmon is near the mouth of the river where it was born, it uses smell as its guide to find that river. But we still do not know how a salmon can tell which direction to go when it is too far out at sea to pick up the smell of the river. Some people think the position of the sun tells the salmon which way to go. Others say the fish may have something in its body that works like a magnet.

At the beginning of their fourth year Pacific salmon start heading back to the river where they were born.

4

Some think that they find their direction from the position of the sun.

Some scientists believe that salmon have something like a magnet to tell them which direction is north.

I've got a secret!

It's strange! How in the world do they know?

Although we are not sure how they know it, it seems certain that salmon know where they are even in the middle of the huge ocean.

● To the Parent

The general term salmon includes both Atlantic salmon (*Salmo salar*) and Pacific salmon (*Oncorhynchus*). Both types of salmon hatch in rivers, then go downstream to the ocean, and return to their native rivers as adults to spawn. Scientists are not sure how salmon know which way to head in the middle of vast oceans. Some believe that salmon can tell direction from the position of the sun, or that they may determine their location by sensing Earth's magnetic field. When salmon reach coastal waters, they rely on memory to detect the smell of their river of origin.

Why Does the Angler Fish Have a Light?

ANSWER 1

To catch small fish to eat. The small fish are attracted by the light at the end of a "fishing rod" that sticks out of the forehead of the deep-sea angler fish.

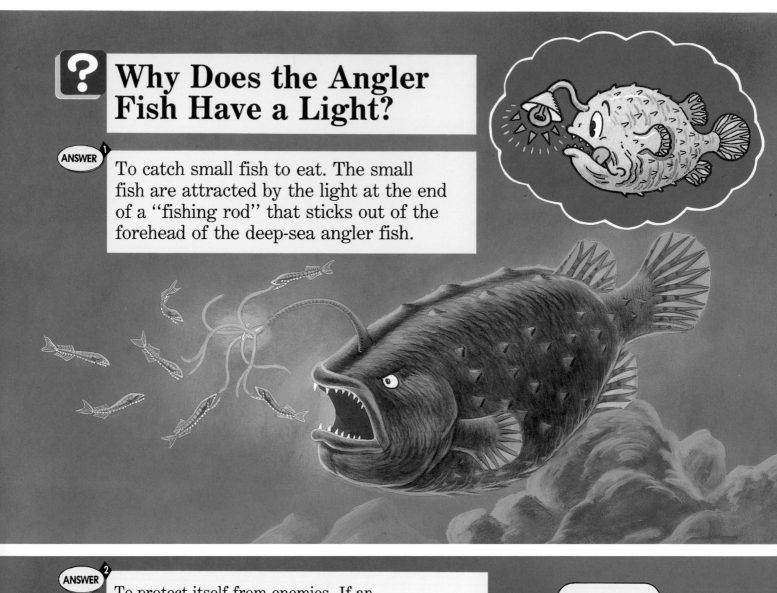

ANSWER 2

To protect itself from enemies. If an enemy approaches, the deep-sea angler fish uses the glowing light on its fishing rod to frighten the attacker.

Boy! Did he get a surprise!

Do Other Deep-Sea Fish Have Lights?

Some deep-sea fish have a stomach that glows. The sea is lighter toward the surface, so enemies attacking from below cannot see them easily.

The part of the fish that glows depends on what kind of fish it is. In the deep, dark parts of the ocean the glowing lights help to identify other fish of the same species.

Fish of the same species glow in the same way.

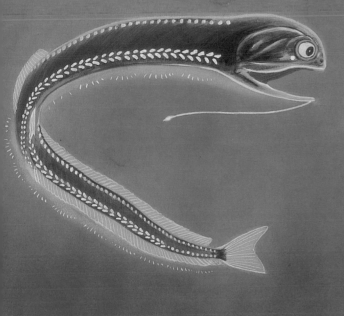

● To the Parent

Bioluminescence is the emission of light by a living organism, such as the light coming from the deep-sea angler fish's lure. The light is the result of a chemical process, the oxidation of the light-producing substance luciferin by the enzyme luciferase, and produces no heat. The light can be used to attract prey; to frighten predators; as camouflage; or for species recognition.

Did You Know That Some Fish Build Nests like Birds' Nests?

(ANSWER) The stickleback uses the stalks and roots of water plants to make a round nest that looks just like some birds' nests. The male stickleback builds the nest and then invites a female into it. The female enters the nest, lays her eggs and swims away. The male then looks after the eggs until they hatch into young fish, called fry. He also looks after the fry until they are old enough to swim away on their own.

That fish's nest is like a bird's nest.

■ The stickleback nest and the male's duties

First he builds a round nest using stalks and roots of water plants.

When the nest is finished, he brings a female back to it to get her to lay her eggs there.

The female goes into the nest and lays her eggs inside it.

■ On guard

The stickleback's nest of branches and plants is complete. There are eggs inside the nest.

Male stickleback ▶ protecting his nest

Circle shows eggs ▶

If another male or an enemy approaches, the nest builder chases it away.

Finally the eggs hatch, and the fry swim around close to the nest.

● To the Parent

Members of the stickleback family are characterized by a row of spines on the back, in front of the dorsal fin. Sticklebacks are found in both fresh and salt water. In spring and early summer the male stickleback builds a nest. The female lays 20 to 30 eggs in the nest at one time. The male then fertilizes the eggs in the nest. The male has a strong territorial instinct and does not allow enemies or rival males to approach his nest. He protects the eggs and later the young.

How Do Archerfish Catch Prey?

ANSWER Archerfish catch insects by shooting them with water. They can make their mouth into the shape of a tube and shoot water out of it in a powerful jet, much like a water pistol.

An archerfish shoots water at a caterpillar on a leaf.

Watch out, caterpillar!

How an Archerfish Catches Its Dinner

First it spots a juicy caterpillar and takes aim.

Then it shoots a jet of water from its mouth.

The caterpillar falls into the water and is eaten.

● **To the Parent**

Archerfish is the name given to the five species of fresh- and saltwater Indo-Pacific fishes that make up the family Toxotidae. They are named for their ability to shoot a jet of water to knock down insects off leaves above the water's surface. In an archerfish's upper jaw is a narrow groove. By pressing its tongue up against the roof of its mouth, the archerfish can turn this groove into a tube. It then uses its gill flaps to pressurize the water and shoot it out through its mouth. It has an excellent aim and rarely misses its prey.

Do Electric Eels Really Make Electricity?

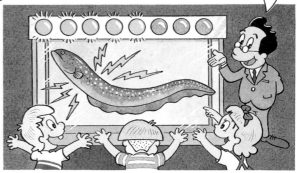

It turns on all these lights.

ANSWER Yes, they certainly do! Their bodies can produce a very strong jolt of electricity. In some aquariums you can see demonstrations of how electric eels produce enough power to turn lights on. They can shock whatever is swimming in the water around them.

I'd better watch out. I don't want to get shocked!

▲ **An electric eel.** It is 8 feet (2.4 m) long and lives in rivers in South America.

Why Does It Produce Electricity?

The electric eel uses electricity as a weapon to catch food and to protect itself from its enemies. It can produce a jolt of electricity strong enough to give a severe shock to anything nearby. The eel also gives off a lower amount of electricity all the time, using it like radar to detect the underwater objects in its surroundings.

It protects itself from enemies by giving them a strong shock.

It paralyses small fish with a shock and then eats them.

The electric eel cannot see very well, so it uses electricity to help it avoid obstacles in the water.

Other Fish That Produce Electricity

▲ **Electric catfish.** It lives in African rivers and ponds.

▲ **Electric ray.** It lives in the oceans.

? How Do Frogs and Toads Catch Food with Their Tongue?

ANSWER Their tongue is very sticky, and they can shoot it out a long, long way. If they see an insect that they want, they shoot out their long tongue and catch it.

▲ A toad sees something to eat.

▲ First the toad shoots out its sticky tongue to catch the insect. Next it will roll up its tongue and eat the insect stuck on the end.

A Frog Will Try to Catch Anything That Moves

Frogs like to eat insects that are living. If they see something that is moving and looks as if it will fit inside their mouth, they will try to catch it. Sometimes, though, they make a mistake and try to swallow the wrong thing.

Frogs will catch only things that are moving.

If an insect does not move, the frog will not touch it.

Ha! I'll fool him. I'll just play dead.

MINI-DATA

Sometimes a frog will attack a blade of grass waving in the wind because it thinks the grass is something to eat. It might attack a river fern stalk that grows near water. If you shake a stalk of grass in front of a frog, the frog will think the tip is something to eat and will try to catch it.

■ A frog that's made a mistake

▲ A leopard frog catches a crayfish.

▲ The frog is surprised to have its tongue pinched by the crayfish's claw, and it spits the crayfish out.

● To the Parent

When a frog or toad spots a moving insect that it wants to eat, it quickly leaps forward and at the same time opens its large mouth and flicks out its tongue. On the end of the tongue of most types of frogs and toads are two small protrusions, which are wrapped around the prey being captured. Most frogs and toads eat insects, other small arthropods and worms. But a number of the larger species, such as the large North American bullfrog, also eat other frogs and toads, small rodents and small reptiles.

Why Does a Lizard's Tail Break Off?

ANSWER A lizard's tail breaks very easily. If an enemy catches it, the tail breaks off and the lizard can get away.

■ The breaking point

The lizard's tail has a built-in breaking point near its rear end.

The lizard's tail can break off at this point.

A severed tail. It is not very painful.

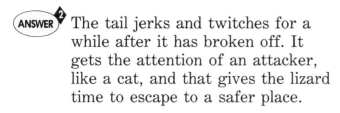

ANSWER 2 The tail jerks and twitches for a while after it has broken off. It gets the attention of an attacker, like a cat, and that gives the lizard time to escape to a safer place.

● **To the Parent**

Some lizards have a built-in snap-off point in their tail. When the lizard is caught by the tail, the tail breaks off. This self-amputation, a process called autotomy, allows the lizard to escape from the attacker. The severed tail continues to move, diverting the attacker's attention while the lizard runs away to safety. A new tail begins growing, or regenerating, immediately and reaches normal size within a few months.

Now's your chance to get away, while the cat's looking at the tail.

What Happens After the Tail Breaks Off?

A new tail grows in place of the old one. This is called regeneration.

▲ **Lizard with its original tail.** If the tail has never been broken off, it can be very long.

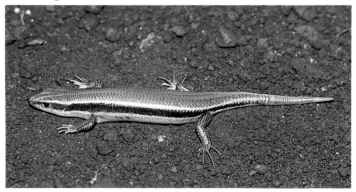

▲ **Lizard with a regenerated tail.** A new tail has grown, but it will take some time for it to grow long.

? Did You Know That One Lizard Can Run on Water?

ANSWER The basilisk lizard can run across the water. It takes a step with its left foot before the right one can sink, then takes the next step with its right foot before the left foot sinks. The lizard does not sink because its body is very light and because it spreads the toes of its back feet extremely wide to keep them from sinking.

The secret is here on the bottom.

▲ Scales spread between the toes of the back feet.

When the basilisk runs on the water it has to move very quickly to keep from sinking.

● **To the Parent**

The basilisk lizard will run on its hind legs for short distances across the surface of the water to escape from an enemy. The basilisk is able to stay on top of the water because it can spread the toes of its hind feet. When the toes are spread, elongated scales on the sides of the toes increase the total surface area of the feet. The surface tension of the water is then sufficient to support the lizard as it moves quickly. The basilisk can also swim, and can remain submerged for long periods.

A basilisk races over ▶ the surface, splashing water as it goes.

Why Do Turtles Come Up on Land?

ANSWER If you go to visit a pond or stream on a warm, sunny day you may find turtles that have come up onto land. Sometimes they climb onto rocks and fallen trees. They do this to sunbathe so they can warm up.

They look heavy.

▲ **Turtles basking in the sun**

Why Do They Want to Sunbathe?

Just like you, turtles need sunshine in order for their bodies to make vitamin D. Vitamin D is what makes our bones strong. And it makes turtles' shells strong too.

Drying out in the sun helps turtles to get rid of any plants or animals that have become attached to their bodies.

The main reason that turtles come out of the water to sunbathe, though, is to warm up their bodies. When they are cold, they feel sluggish and do not want to move around much. After they warm up, they feel active again.

Too much of a good thing

Turtles need sunlight. But if they stay in the sun too long and get too warm, the turtles will not feel well. So once they have had enough sun, they must go back into the water.

Why Do Sea Turtles Leave the Water to Lay Their Eggs?

(ANSWER) They cannot get oxygen from the water the way fish can. If the sea turtle's eggs hatched underwater the baby turtles would drown right away. In fact if a sea turtle laid her eggs in the sea, they would die even before they could hatch. That would happen because even the eggs need air to breathe. So that is why sea turtles leave the water to lay their eggs.

This is awful! I can't breathe!

■ Red sea turtle laying her eggs

Look at all those eggs!

When it is time for the sea turtle to lay her eggs she leaves the water and crawls up onto the beach. She digs a hole in the sand, and there she lays her eggs.

The female sea turtle digs a hole about 16 inches (40 cm) deep and lays about 120 eggs.

She digs the hole with her back legs.

▲ **Sea turtle laying her eggs**

When she has finished she uses her back legs to fill up the hole with sand and cover the eggs.

The Turtle's Life Cycle

The baby turtles that have just hatched begin to move toward the sea as soon as they can crawl out of the nest. The sea is where they will grow up. When the females are grown and ready to lay eggs themselves they will return to the beach.

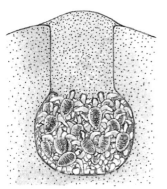

The eggs hatch after about two months.

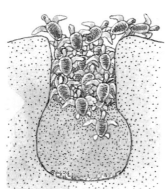

The baby turtles all leave the nest together.

Their enemies are seagulls and crabs.

▲ Baby turtles crawl toward the sea. They start for the water as soon as they come out of the nest.

The turtles grow into adults in warm ocean waters. When it is time to lay eggs they return to land.

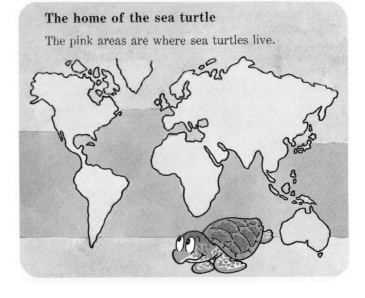

The home of the sea turtle

The pink areas are where sea turtles live.

● **To the Parent**

Sea turtles are air-breathing reptiles. If their eggs hatched underwater, the baby turtles would drown before they could reach the surface. Actually, if the eggs were laid underwater they would never hatch at all. The turtle embryos must breathe through their shells, or they will not develop. The embryos also need heat. Underwater, it is too cold for them to develop. So the female sea turtle must come up onto dry land to lay her eggs.

Why Do Cranes Stand on One Leg?

(ANSWER) A crane's body is covered almost all over with feathers to keep it warm. But the crane loses heat through its legs because there are no feathers on them. To save as much heat as it can, the crane stands on only one leg and tucks the other one up against its body.

I get cold if I use both feet.

It doesn't fall down

If people try to stand on only one leg with their eyes closed they soon fall down. But cranes can even go to sleep while standing on one leg. They stand on one leg all night long and it does not bother them a bit.

Cranes sleep while standing in an icy river in the winter.

● **To the Parent**

Most birds rest their breast on the ground or a tree branch and tuck their head under one of their wings when they sleep. But cranes and some other water birds often sleep standing in water. They stand on only one leg, tucking the other up against their body, in order to minimize the loss of body heat.

Did You Know That Some Birds' Babies Are Raised by Other Birds?

ANSWER Some birds do not raise their own babies. They have found a way to get other birds to do the work for them. The cuckoo, for instance, lays an egg in a nest belonging to reed warblers. When the cuckoo chick hatches, the reed warblers take care of it.

The cuckoo chick grows larger than an adult reed warbler.

The cuckoo waits for a chance to lay her egg.

▲ **Adult cuckoo**

▲ Even if one of the warblers is there the cuckoo shoves their eggs out.

▲ The cuckoo waits until both warbler parents are away from the nest, then moves in and lays an egg.

The cuckoo takes one of the warblers' eggs and replaces it by laying one of her own eggs.

▲ The cuckoo's egg is a little larger than the others.

▲ The cuckoo chick that has just hatched shoves all the reed warblers' eggs out of the nest.

▲ The young cuckoo gets all the food, so it grows larger than its foster parents.

Birds Raised by Others

Here are some birds that get
other birds to raise their young.

Paradise whydah

Honey guide

Common cuckoo

Chinese hawk cuckoo

●To the Parent

One of the most unusual phenomena in the animal world is the
parasitic instinct of some birds, known as brood parasites, that do
not build nests of their own but lay their eggs in other birds' nests,
leaving the eggs to be cared for by the other birds. The cuckoo is
one of these. Its chick hatches before the other eggs in the host
nest and shoves the other eggs out. This instinctive action by the
cuckoo chick occurs even when the foster parents are in the nest.

❓ Why Do Some Birds Migrate?

(ANSWER) We say that birds migrate when they leave one area and fly to another. They may migrate because a place becomes too cold for them or there is no longer enough food. When the seasons change and there is more food the birds fly back to their first homes.

When the place they were born gets too cold birds begin migrating.

Back in their birthplace again, they build nests and raise their young.

The migrating birds leave home and fly south.

After spending the winter in the south, the migrating birds fly back to their homes in the north.

In the south birds find much warmer weather and more food than in the places they left behind.

When the seasons change and the place they came from is warm again, the birds begin their return migration.

Note: The arrows on the map are only symbolic representations of the north-south routes that migrating birds usually follow.

How Far Do Birds Travel When They Migrate?

Some birds fly much farther than others. The bird that is best known for migrating long distances is the arctic tern. When winter approaches the tern leaves its birthplace near the North Pole and migrates to Antarctica, almost all the way to the South Pole.

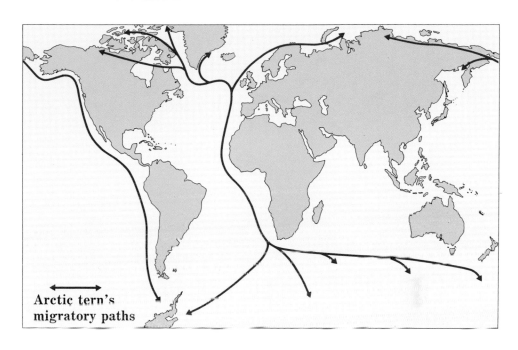

Arctic tern's migratory paths

Cranes That Cross the Himalayas

▲ This photo shows cranes passing over Mount Manaslu in the Himalayas.

Cranes that migrate from Siberia to India have to cross the Himalayas, the world's highest mountains. They have to fly very high, where there is little oxygen.

● To the Parent

Migration refers to the annual round trip that many birds, fish and other animals make in response to seasonal changes in their food supply. Almost half of the world's birds migrate, some of them long distances. The champion of the long-distance travellers is the arctic tern, which nests in the northern polar regions. During the eight months in which the arctic tern is not nesting, its migratory flight to and from Antarctica may cover nearly 24,000 miles (38,600 km).

? Why Does the Male Bowerbird Decorate His Nest So Carefully?

ANSWER The male bowerbird gathers brush to build a nest, called a bower. He decorates his home with whatever he can find. He will mate with a female in the bower, but first he has to attract her by having a very beautiful bower. That is why he spends a lot of time building and decorating it.

Come and be my mate.

▲ Male bowerbird

▲ The bowerbird builds his bower on the ground and decorates it with anything colourful that he can find.

▲ When the male has finished decorating his bower, here using plastic and other things, he invites a female in.

▲ The female's colours are different.

■ The courtship

The male performs a mating dance in front of his bower as he tries to attract the female.

● **To the Parent**

A male bowerbird builds and decorates a structure called a bower to attract a female. The male will collect feathers, plastic and various other colourful objects with which to decorate his bower. When the bower is finished the male bowerbird calls a female and attempts to attract her favour by dancing in front of the bower and pointing out its fine features with his beak. If the female is impressed, she enters the bower and mates with its builder. After they mate, the female goes away and builds her own nest, in which she lays her eggs. There are 20 different species of bowerbirds, all found in Australia and New Guinea. The design of the bower built by a male bowerbird varies according to species.

❓ Why Does This Bird Build a Big Mound?

ANSWER The mallee fowl builds a mound so that its eggs will hatch. The male makes a very large mound out of dead leaves, sand and earth. Then the female lays eggs in the mound. As the leaves rot they produce heat, keeping the eggs warm so they will hatch.

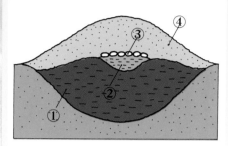

Inside view of the mound

Leaves that were gathered and put into the mallee's mound four or five months ago have already rotted.

The male controls the temperature of the eggs by making the covering of sand thicker or thinner.

① These leaves have already rotted.

② Fresh leaves cushion the eggs.

③ Eggs were laid some days apart.

④ Sand controls the temperature.

■ The mallee fowl tends his nest

The male digs a hole in the rotted leaves and then adds some new leaves, on which the female begins laying eggs.

The male covers the eggs with sand or earth so that the heat won't escape. The mound grows higher and higher.

▲ **Red mallee fowl.** Shown here in the inset circle, it has built its mound in the forest.

By adjusting the thickness of the layer of sand the male is able to keep the mound at a constant temperature.

● **To the Parent**

Mound builders, which include scrub fowl, brush turkeys and mallee fowl, are distributed over Indonesia, New Guinea and Australia. Mound builders do not use their own body heat to incubate their eggs. In the case of the Australian red mallee fowl, the male builds a huge mound that serves as an incubator. He begins in the autumn, digging a hole about 10 feet (3 m) across and 3 feet (0.9 m) deep, then putting fallen leaves in it. The leaves decompose to form a compost that generates heat. In early spring the male digs a hole in the top of the heap of compost and adds new leaves to make a nest. About a month later, over a period of several days, the female lays her eggs there and the male covers them with sand. During the 90 days before the eggs hatch the male monitors the mound's interior temperature, which he maintains at a constant 91° Fahrenheit (33° C.) by adjusting the sand's thickness. After hatching, the young burrow out on their own.

? Why Do a Chipmunk's Cheeks Puff Out?

ANSWER A chipmunk can puff out its cheeks to hold lots of acorns and other things it likes to eat. That is the way the chipmunk carries its food.

That's convenient.

■ Cheek pouches

The chipmunk's cheeks are like a basket for holding things. The cheeks form pouches, which can be stuffed full of food.

▲ Its pouches are empty.

▲ Its pouches are full.

56

Where Do They Take the Acorns?

The chipmunks carry the acorns to their burrow or to places near the burrow. Then they dig holes and bury them. The acorns are what the chipmunks eat while they rest in their burrow in the winter.

When winter comes and snow falls they won't be able to find any food. But they can eat the acorns they've stored up during the autumn.

With its cheek pouches full of acorns, the chipmunk digs a hole.

It stores the nuts in the hole so that other animals will not get them.

The chipmunk carefully fills the hole and then pats the earth down with its paws.

■ The winter burrow

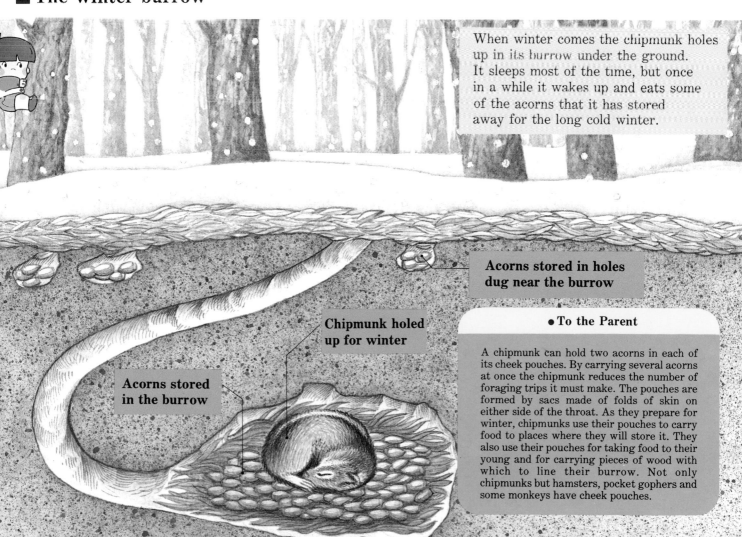

When winter comes the chipmunk holes up in its burrow under the ground. It sleeps most of the time, but once in a while it wakes up and eats some of the acorns that it has stored away for the long cold winter.

Acorns stored in holes dug near the burrow

Chipmunk holed up for winter

Acorns stored in the burrow

● To the Parent

A chipmunk can hold two acorns in each of its cheek pouches. By carrying several acorns at once the chipmunk reduces the number of foraging trips it must make. The pouches are formed by sacs made of folds of skin on either side of the throat. As they prepare for winter, chipmunks use their pouches to carry food to places where they will store it. They also use their pouches for taking food to their young and for carrying pieces of wood with which to line their burrow. Not only chipmunks but hamsters, pocket gophers and some monkeys have cheek pouches.

? Did You Know That Prairie Dogs Build Their Own Town?

ANSWER Families of prairie dogs burrow in the ground to make tunnels and nests. Since many families burrow in the same area, they build what looks like a large town of prairie dogs.

A Town with a Very Good View

Prairie dogs eat all the grass near their burrows so that they will have a better view of what is around them.

With all the grass removed the sentries can spot coyotes or any other enemies that might come near their home.

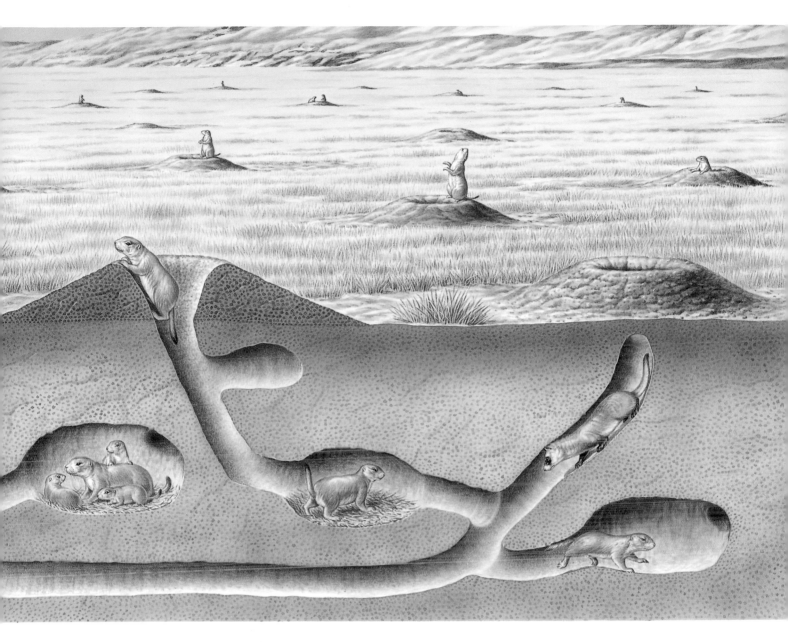

The Prairie Dog's Real Enemy

The badger preys on prairie dogs but cannot go farther than the opening of the burrow. But a weasel is thin enough to get into the burrow and attack.

● To the Parent

Prairie dogs are small burrowing rodents whose call is something like a dog barking. They are found in the plains of North America. A family of prairie dogs usually is made up of a male, several females and a number of young. Such a family is known as a coterie, and a number of coteries close together form a town. Some towns may cover as much as 160 acres (65 ha). Prairie dogs eat all of the grass, especially any tall grass, in the vicinity of their mound-like burrow entrances. This eliminates all cover for predators, which can then be spotted in time for the prairie dogs to escape to the safety of their burrows. The prairie dogs' greatest enemy is the black-footed weasel, which is thin enough to get inside their burrows and attack them. The elevated burrow entrances also prevent flooding of the burrows.

Why Do Bats Hang Upside Down?

ANSWER A bat's body is well suited to flying. The back legs are very thin. They are connected by a thin skin that helps the bat fly. But the thin legs and the connecting skin make it hard for the bat to stand. That is why you always see bats hanging upside down.

▲ A baby bat clings to its upside-down mother.

The bat's wings have the same kind of bone structure as a person's arms. The legs are very thin. At the ends of a bat's legs there are claws.

You'll see when you compare the places that have the same numbers.

■ A bat's body

A bat's wing and a person's hand have the same number of fingers.

Bat wing ▶

Human arm ▶

Back leg. It is weak and thin.

Toes. They have claws at the end.

■ It's easy to fly from a high place

A bat can fly off whenever it wants if it is hanging upside down.

But it is much harder to take off from the ground.

One thing it doesn't do upside down!

Because its back legs are so thin and weak, a bat can't stand up.

⁇ But How Do They Go to the Toilet?

The bat pulls itself up and hangs by its claws so that its rear end is pointing downward.

It uses its claws to pull itself upright.

Once the bat is turned upright, waste drops between its legs.

● To the Parent

Bats are mammals. They are warm-blooded, covered in fur and they suckle their young. They also have wings and can fly. While a bird's wing is made of feathers, a bat's wing is formed from a thin membrane supported by the long finger bones, or digits, of the foreleg. A membrane also extends between the tail and the hind legs to help the bat fly. The bat's body is well suited to flying but not to walking or running.

? Why Do Beavers Build Dams?

(ANSWER) Beavers build a dam to stop up a river and form a pond. When a lot of water has backed up in the pond they build nests that look like small islands. With nests in the middle of the pond, beavers are safe from their enemies.

The entrance to the nest is hidden under the water's surface.

Beaver nest

Entrance

How the Dam and Nest Are Built

The beaver begins by building a dam of branches and mud in a stream. Water backs up behind the dam.

The beaver also uses branches and mud to build its nest out in the pond that is forming behind the dam.

■ A beaver cuts down a tree

A beaver has very strong teeth. It can cut down even a large tree by gnawing away at it.

It gnaws branches off the fallen tree, carries them to the pond and uses them to make its nest and dam.

The beaver eats some of the bark and leaves and stores some of it to eat when winter comes.

Dam

Food stored for winter

When the nest is finished and the pond has risen, the entrance is well hidden under the surface of the water.

● To the Parent

Beavers live in the water in the sub-arctic forests of North America and near the Elbe and Rhône rivers of Europe. Trees like the poplar and the birch are sources of food and building materials for the beaver. The animal constructs a dam of logs, branches and mud to block the flow of a river so that a pond will be formed. In the pond the beaver builds a nest called a lodge, which can be entered only from below the water. The depth of the water is regulated to hide the entrance without covering the lodge's floor.

? What Do Foxes Use Their Tail For?

ANSWER 1 A mother fox uses her tail as a signal for her pups to follow. The tip of a fox's tail is white. When the mother fox raises her tail it is very easy for the small foxes to see it. They can follow her easily without getting lost.

■ Animal tail signals

Golden cat. The fur on the bottom part of the golden cat's tail is white. That makes this signal easy to see even in the dark.

Deer. When a deer raises its tail it shows the white fur on its rump. White fur stands out, making this signal very easy to see.

ANSWER 2 The fox uses its tail to help keep its balance when it is running and has to make a sharp turn. It also uses that bushy tail the way we would use a scarf, to wrap itself up and keep warm in cold weather.

It's gone to sleep.

In cold weather the fox curls up and covers its face with its tail. This keeps heat from escaping, so the fox stays warm.

A running fox uses its tail for balance when making a sharp turn. That way its body won't tip over too far and it can make a smooth turn.

MINI-DATA

Other animals that have their own scarf

Chipmunk

Dormouse

Chipmunks and dormice also use their tails as scarfs to keep warm when they are asleep.

Wart hog. The mother and young wart hog hold their long tails straight up when they run. So this signal is like a flag in the air.

● **To the Parent**

Some animals use their tail as a signalling device so that members of a herd or a mother and her young will not get separated. Within a herd, a raised tail also can signal danger. The tail often has white fur on it so that it can be seen easily even in thick undergrowth or in the dark. Animals that have to chase nimble prey use their tail to keep their balance when they suddenly change direction. In the winter, when their fur grows thicker, some animals use their tail like a muffler to keep warm.

How Do Sea Otters Open Seashells?

ANSWER Because it knows how to use rocks as tools the sea otter is able to eat shellfish. The sea otter turns over onto its back, places a rock on its stomach and then breaks a seashell on the rock. Even the hardest shell will break if it is banged against the rock over and over again.

Breaking a shell
The otter brings the shell down with a splash.

■ Catching its food

It digs in the sandy sea bottom until it finds a shellfish.

It uses a rock to break an abalone loose from a ledge it is clinging to.

■ Picking up a rock

Holding the shell under its front paw it swims to the surface with the rock.

Wow! That looks hard!

Animals That Use Tools

Most animals and birds do not use tools, but there are some that do.

A chimpanzee sticks a straw into a termite nest and then eats the termites that cling to the straw.

When an Egyptian vulture wants to eat an ostrich egg it drops a rock on the egg to break it.

■ Using its stomach as a table

After it has broken the shell open, the otter uses its stomach as a table and eats the meat inside the shell.

A woodpecker finch uses a cactus spine or a small twig to pick small insects out of a tree.

❓ What Do Deer Use Their Antlers For?

(ANSWER) Only the males have antlers. As the mating season gets closer, males lock horns and push each other around. They compete this way to show which one is stronger. The winner gets to mate with a female.

The males lock horns and do battle.

●To the Parent

The male deer, or buck, has a set of horns called antlers. Every year he sheds his antlers and grows new ones. Young bucks have small antlers, but by the time a buck is four years old he grows a full-sized set of horns. In the spring and summer the antlers are soft and are covered with a velvety skin. By the autumn the antlers have hardened and the skin has peeled off. During the mating season bucks use their antlers in combat to compete with one another. The victorious buck drives away his rivals, establishes his territory and then mates with whichever doe enters it.

How the Antlers Change

In spring the antlers begin to grow, covered with a soft skin like velvet. As spring turns to summer the antlers grow larger. In autumn the skin drops off and the deer has strong, hard antlers with sharp points. In winter the antlers drop off at the roots.

Spring

Oh, too bad!

The loser must leave the territory.

The winner gets to mate with a doe.

Antlers and Age

The antlers grow differently each year. As a buck gets older his antlers have more points.

First year

Autumn of second year

Autumn of third year

Autumn of fourth year

Early summer

Late summer

❓ Why Does a Hare's Fur Change Colour?

ANSWER Many hares have fur that is brown in summer but white in winter. Snow falls in winter and everything is covered in white. With white fur it is easier for a hare to hide from its enemies. In summer it is easier for the hare to hide if it has brown fur. The fur changes colour so that the hare can always blend in.

■ How the hare's coat changes colour

From summer to the middle of autumn its coat is brown.

The hare has both a summer coat and a winter coat.

About mid-autumn the hare starts losing its brown fur and growing white fur to replace it.

By winter the hare's coat is completely white except for the tips of its ears, which are always black.

They change colour so they can blend in with their surroundings.

The Secret of White Fur

White fur is hollow. As well as blending in with snow, this kind of fur keeps the hare warm in the winter.

▲ **Snowshoe hare.** Its coat is the same colour as the snow.

Brown hair is not hollow at the centre. It lets body heat escape much faster.

Hollow hair has air inside it, and that makes it harder for body heat to escape.

Animals That Turn White in Winter

Summer   Winter

Ermine

Summer   Winter

Pygmy weasel

Summer   Winter

Ptarmigan

● **To the Parent**

Hares living in the cold northern latitudes have white fur in the winter and darker, usually greyish brown, fur in the summer. The winter coat appears white because the hairs lack the pigments that colour the summer coat. The hairs of the winter coat are hollow and filled with air. With air filling their centres the hairs provide insulation that conserves body heat and keeps the hare warm. In warmer parts of the world hares are one colour all year round.

Do Bears Really Sleep All Winter Long?

(ANSWER) Bears sleep through most of the winter in protected places such as caves, hollow trees or holes that they dig beneath trees. But they may wake up if disturbed. On mild winter days, they will even come out of their warm dens to look for food.

Looks like he's comfortable!

How Bears Sleep through the Winter

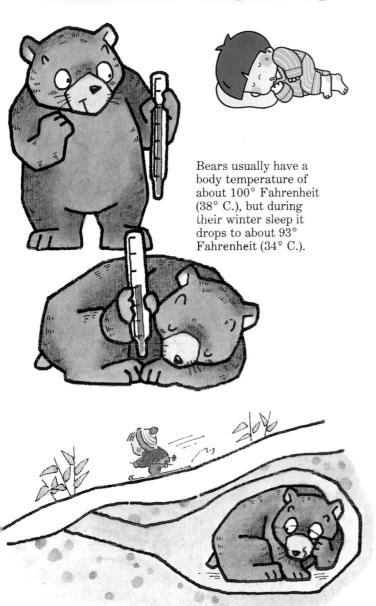

Bears usually have a body temperature of about 100° Fahrenheit (38° C.), but during their winter sleep it drops to about 93° Fahrenheit (34° C.).

▲ **A sleepy bear.** As the weather warms up in March, the bear wakes up and comes out of its den.

The female gives birth to cubs in her winter den. She usually has twins.

Bears do not sleep very soundly. If they are disturbed by a noise, they may wake up.

Many people say bears hibernate during the winter. But they do not—they just fall into a deep sleep. When an animal really hibernates, the way an Arctic ground squirrel does, its body temperature drops very low and it does not breathe very much.

● **To the Parent**

In hibernation an animal's body temperature drops to the level of the surrounding air temperature and the hibernating animal becomes almost completely inactive. Bears are not true hibernators. More precisely, they become dormant in the winter. As they sleep their body temperature seldom drops below 88° Fahrenheit (31° C.). They may occasionally wake up and move about, and the females nurse their cubs. Bears prepare for their winter sleep by gaining weight in the autumn.

Why Do Orang-utans Have Long Arms?

ANSWER Orang-utans spend most of their life in the trees of tropical forests. They seldom come down to the ground. As they move around in the trees they hold on to the branches. With their long arms it is easy for them to move from one branch to the next. Their long arms also help them reach for the seeds and nuts they like to eat.

74

Down here I have to walk.

Life in the Trees

The gibbon uses its long arms to move rapidly through the treetops. It moves quickly, one hand over the other.

The spider monkey uses not only its long arms and legs but also its very long tail as it swings quickly from tree to tree.

● **To the Parent**

The orang-utan is one of the anthropoid, or man-like, apes and is found on the islands of Borneo and Sumatra in Southeast Asia. It normally lives in trees, but on the rare occasions when it comes down to the ground it walks on all fours. The orang-utan is distinguished by the way it clenches its hind feet into fists as it walks. The chimpanzee and the gorilla are also anthropoid apes, but they live primarily on the ground and keep their hind feet flat when they walk. Like orang-utans, most apes and monkeys that live and move about freely in the trees have long arms to help them grasp branches as they travel through the forest.

? Can Dolphins Talk?

(ANSWER) Dolphins constantly cry out to other dolphins, but these cries are not really the same thing as what we call talking. They can't discuss difficult problems with one another in the same way that people can. But dolphins do seem to have a sort of language that is made up of several different kinds of sounds. They can make sounds to call one another together, for instance, or to tell one another where food is.

There's some nice squid over there.

MINI-DATA

Signals are sent out from here

Melon

Signals return here and go to the ear

The whistles, clicks and other sounds made by a dolphin come from nasal passages in its forehead. A lump of fat called the melon focuses the outgoing sound signals into a beam. The dolphin receives incoming sound signals through its lower jaw.

● **To the Parent**

Dolphins are aquatic mammals found throughout the world's oceans. The sounds they make can be divided into two main types. One is a system of whistles and other cries used to communicate with other dolphins. The other type is a range of high-frequency clicks that dolphins use like sonar to survey their surroundings as they navigate. Both types emanate from the nasal passages in the dolphin's forehead.

Sometimes we can hear their cries when they're above the surface. When they're underwater we can't.

Peep!

Hey, Mummy, wait for me!

❓ What Are These Animals Doing?

Look! This is a fish, but it can live outside the water.

◀ This mudskipper has climbed up onto a tree. It leaves the water to eat shellfish stranded by low tide. It uses its fins to get around.

◀ This filefish is looking for something to eat. The filefish blows the sand and stirs it up as it looks for things hiding there.

▲ A puddingwife hides itself in the sand.

◀ This puddingwife is sleeping. Before it goes to sleep the puddingwife covers itself with sand like a blanket. Fish have no eyelids, so their eyes stay open when they are asleep.

Here we see a striped cleaner shrimp eating tiny parasites from a fish's body. The fish does not move until the cleaning job is finished.

I thought it was eating the fish!

This round mask crab is holding up a shell to hide itself so that its enemies will not see it. Everywhere these crabs go they carry a shell around with them. They use it like a mask or a disguise, or to hide behind.

The pink sea anemone usually fastens itself to something hard like a rock. But when it wants to move it lets go and swims away.

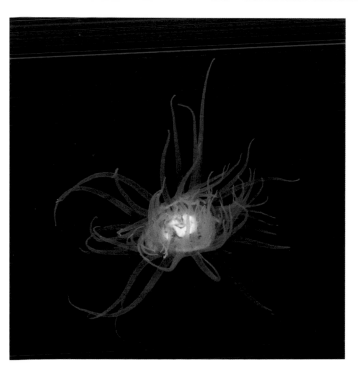

This sea anemone can swim along the same way a jellyfish does.

● **To the Parent**

The mudskipper is an amphibious fish that lives on tidal flatlands. It uses its strong pectoral fins to move about on land, where it breathes through water trapped in its gill chambers. Most sea anemones do not swim, remaining anchored to a solid object such as a rock. They creep along slowly if they move at all. But the swimming sea anemone and the pink sea anemone can swim.

Whose Beak Is This?

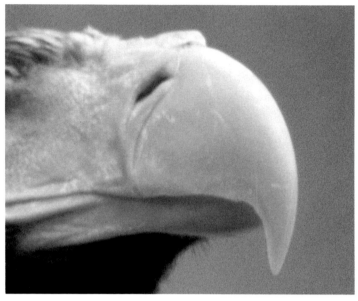

■ The sea eagle's

The eagle's beak has a sharp hook at the end to tear apart the flesh of the animals it eats.

■ The Caribbean flamingo's

The flamingo puts its beak into the water and filters out tiny plants and animals to eat.

■ The toucan's

The toucan's colourful beak is large and looks very heavy. But actually the beak is spongy inside, making it very lightweight.

• **To the Parent**

The sharply curved beak of carnivorous birds such as the sea eagle is very useful in tearing apart the flesh of their prey. The flamingo's beak has a sieve-like structure on the inside that enables the bird to filter a meal of plankton out of the water. The bulk of a toucan's beak is made up of a porous substance with many pockets of air, so the beak is not as heavy as it might appear.

Growing-Up Album

Who Is Talking?

All the animals on these pages are talking, but which one is saying what? Look at the words they have said, then find the animals that said them. Trace a line with your finger to connect each animal with what it said.

1.
I spin my web
and wait for insects.

Hare

Frog

Electric eel

Orang-utan

Butterfly

5.
I have shellfish
for my dinner.

6.
I'll eat any kind
of grass at all.

7.
I use electricity
to catch fish.

Which Are the Real Shadows?

On these two pages you see pictures of four animals. There are a lot of shadows here, too. Look carefully and find the shadows that belong to those four animals.

① ② ③ ④ ⑤ ⑥

Answers Sparrow—15; Bat—8; Crane—13; Fox—7

Where Do They Live?

On the bottom of these two pages you see pictures of six animals. Which ones live in the ocean and which ones live in the pond? See if you can match them to the outlines of animals shown in the ocean and pond pictures.

Ocean

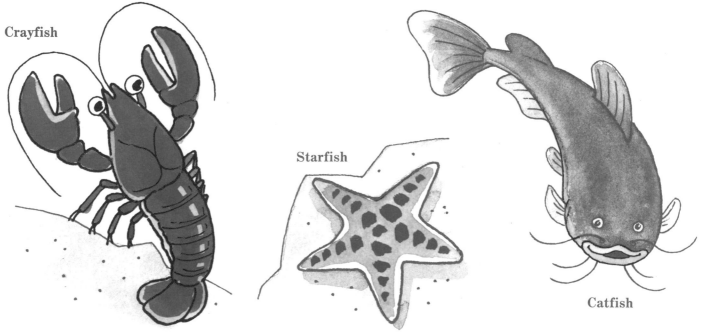

Crayfish

Starfish

Catfish

Pond

Sea urchin

Frog

Octopus

Answers Ocean—sea urchin, octopus, starfish; Pond—crayfish, frog, catfish

A Child's First Library of Learning

Animals in Action

Adapted from Gakken's "Why? Why?"

Original English translation by:
**International Editorial Services Inc.
Tokyo, Japan**

English-language edition (Asia) published by:
Time Life Asia

President,
Time Life International: John D. Hall
VP Time Life International,
Managing Director, Asia: Trevor E. Lunn
CFO and General Manager: Norman Tsoi
Production Supervisor: Stephen Hon
Sales and Marketing
Director: Mushtaq A. Panjwani
New Product Development
Editorial Director: Kate Nussey
Senior Editor: Anne Tseng

New edition:
Project Manager: Kay Halsey
Project Editor: Andrew Bullard
Senior Editor: Katherine K. Rothschild
Publishing Coordinator: Hiroko Wilde

ISBN 0-8094-7275-9

**First published 1988. New edition 1996
Reprinted 2002. Printed in China**

Photo credits: Front cover-Dieter & Mary Plage/Survival/Oxford Scientific Films